Eglantyne Jebb

saves the children

Dorothy Nicolle

Illustrations by

Peter Clayton

Phot… …on

Blue Hills Press

Published by Blue Hills Press
32 Chapel Street, Wem, Shropshire SY4 5ER
www.bluehillspress.co.uk

ISBN 978-0-9560293-4-8

The author is grateful to the Shropshire Regimental Museum in Shrewsbury for permission to use the photograph on page 14. This shows soldiers from the King's Shropshire Light Infantry resting after returning from the trenches in 1917.

Eglantyne Jebb saves the children

Contents

Some words in the book are shown in blue, **like this**, and are explained in the Glossary.

Eglantyne Jebb

1876 - 1928

Eglantyne Jebb grows up

Eglantyne Jebb was born in Shropshire. She had five brothers and sisters.

The family lived in a large house near the town of Ellesmere

Eglantyne did not like playing with dolls.

She was a tomboy - she loved climbing trees, riding her horse in the countryside, swimming in the lake in summer and skating on it in winter.

She also liked to play at soldiers with her brothers and sisters.

This photograph shows Eglantyne, in the middle, with her governess and sister

The house where Eglantyne grew up

Eglantyne never went to school but, instead, she was taught at home by a governess and by her Aunt Bun.

Eglantyne enjoyed writing. She thought she would like to be a war correspondent when she grew up.

When she was twelve Eglantyne wrote a newspaper for the family. It was called “The Briarland Recorder”. She asked all the family to write for it or to draw pictures. The newspaper was filled with articles of all kinds as well as stories and poems. Sometimes she even wrote obituaries when one of their pets died.

Eglantyne goes to university

When she was nineteen, Eglantyne went to Oxford University to study history. In those days very few girls were allowed to go to university and she was lucky that her Aunt Bun helped her to go there.

Eglantyne enjoyed her studies at Oxford and decided that she wanted to be a teacher, helping poor children everywhere.

The children in her classes loved her, but Eglantyne found the work very hard. The classes were very large with around sixty children. Some of the children were naughty and Eglantyne could not control them all.

In the end, she became ill and had to give up teaching.

FREEDOM
FOR
WOMEN
VOTES
FOR
WOMEN

By now her mother was living in Cambridge so Eglantyne went to live with her while she got better.

When she was well again, Eglantyne began to work for a charity in Cambridge helping poor families.

She soon learnt that charity was not just about giving money to people. People needed to be trained so that they could find work or produce food for themselves.

At this time Eglantyne also became interested in politics.

In those days women could not vote in elections. Eglantyne joined the Suffragette Movement demanding “votes for women”. She went on a march; many of the men booed the marchers.

War in the Balkans

In 1912 war broke out in the Balkans. This is part of Europe but, for many years, the countries here had been ruled by the Ottoman Empire. Now the people began to fight for their freedom.

Eglantyne went to the Balkans to help refugees and victims of the war. When she was there she was shocked by the suffering of the children. Many of the children were starving. Many of them were orphans and had nowhere to live. Eglantyne wanted to do everything she could to help them.

A child could be fed with only two pence a day. But first the money needed to be raised.

On her return to England, Eglantyne worked hard to raise the money to help the refugee children.

The First World War

Then, in 1914, the First World War began. People from countries all around the world were soon fighting each other.

Soldiers resting after battle, France, 1917

Because she had seen the suffering of all the people, and especially the children, in the Balkan Wars, Eglantyne became a pacifist.

While the fighting was taking place Eglantyne was in England.

She wrote articles for magazines about all the problems caused by the war.

She wrote about how people were starving all over Europe. She wrote about how prisoners should be treated and the terrible things that were happening all around the world.

She also wrote about ideas on how to prevent wars in the future.

Fight the Famine

After four years the war ended. But the suffering did not stop. In fact, during the first winter after the war things got even worse.

Children were starving all over Europe, and especially in Germany and Austria. Many people did not care about how people in those countries were suffering because they had been Britain's enemies.

But Eglantyne Jebb said that "all wars are waged against children" and "how can a child be your enemy?"

Before the war had even ended Eglantyne had begun a "Fight the Famine" campaign. This was to help all people, but Eglantyne wanted to help children most of all.

Some children were so poor that they had to wear clothes made out of paper. In some parts of Europe 800 children were dying every day from starvation or diseases caused by starvation.

So Eglantyne had posters printed to tell people about the starving children and to raise money to help them.

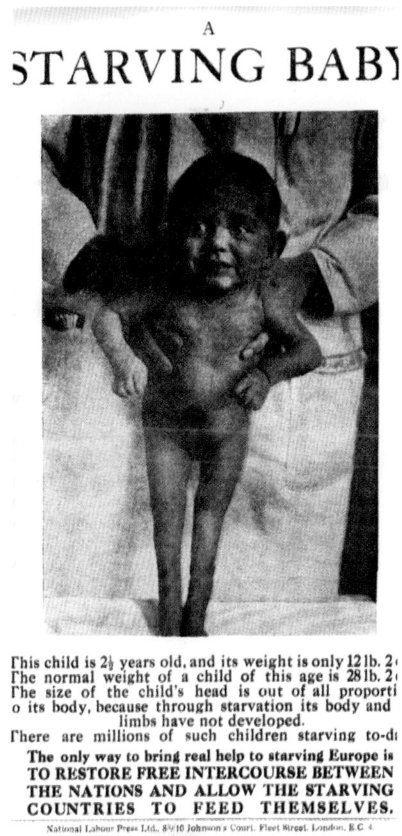

WANTED

One day Eglantyne was arrested for handing out posters about the starving babies without permission.

She was taken to court to be tried. She expected that she would be sent to prison but, instead, the judge fined her five pounds.

After the court case she had tea with the policemen. One of the lawyers gave her a donation to help the children. This paid for her fine. All the newspapers wrote about the court case.

A few days after her trial a meeting was held at the Albert Hall in London to start the Save the Children Fund.

Because of the publicity from the trial, the hall was filled with people who wanted to hear about the Fund.

The
Save the Children Fund

And so, in 1919, the Save the Children Fund was started.

Appeals were made all around the world to raise money to help the children.

In December Eglantyne met the Pope, who is the head of the Roman Catholic Church. The Pope told everyone in the Church that they should give money to the Fund.

Soon other churches, and people of other religions, followed his example.

"The Save the Children Fund pays no regard to politics, race or religion.

A child is a child, whether red, white, brown or black."

At first Eglantyne Jebb just planned to help those children whose lives had been ruined by the First World War. She thought the Fund would only be needed for two years at the most.

But then, in 1921, there was a famine in Russia. Soon afterwards there was a war in Greece. Then, there was an earthquake in Japan.

She realised that there would always be disasters and children who needed help.

And so the Save the Children Fund was here to stay.

Eglantyne dies in Switzerland

Sadly, by the time this happened Eglantyne was already very ill. But she still kept on working.

She gave talks to people about how children around the world were suffering. She wrote many letters asking people to help the Fund.

She worried in case people would lose interest and stop giving money to the Save the Children Fund.

All this hard work made her very weak and, in 1928, she died.

Eglantyne Jebb was buried in Geneva in Switzerland.

By then Eglantyne had set up the Save the Children Fund in many countries around the world.

She had also raised over four million pounds for the charity - that would be like raising twelve million pounds today.

Save the Children today

Today Save the Children helps children in 130 countries in many different ways.

Save the Children has medical teams ready to go anywhere in the world whenever there is the need. In times of famine, or other disasters, they are always there to make sure that the children are fed, clothed and have somewhere safe to stay.

Save the Children has built playgrounds, nurseries and schools in many parts of the world.

Many children are sponsored by the charity so that they can be trained to work and help in the countries where they live.

There are health centres that have been paid for by Save the Children.

Save the Children does so many different kinds of work - in some countries there are even people working to clear landmines to make it safe for the people who live there to work in the fields.

Eglantyne's "Rights of the Child"

Soon after she started The Save the Children Fund Eglantyne Jebb wrote a "Children's Charter". This has now been taken over by the United Nations.

"The only international language is a child's cry."

In her charter Eglantyne wrote down rules for the care of children.

Some of the most important rules are -

* Children must be allowed to develop normally.

* A hungry child should be fed.

* A sick child should be nursed.

* An orphaned child should be looked after.

* In times of distress the child must be helped first.

* All children should be taught to earn a living but should not be exploited.

* Children must be taught to help others.

Glossary

appeal	asking for something you need
article	a piece of writing for a newspaper
charter	a document that lists the rights of people
donation	a gift of money
election	choosing people to run your country
exploit	to use something or someone unfairly
famine	a time when there is little or no food
fine	money paid as a punishment
governess	a teacher in your own home
landmine	a bomb buried under the ground
obituary	a piece in a newspaper about someone who has just died
pacifist	someone who believes all wars are wrong
pay no regard	take no notice of
politics	the work of running the country
publicity	information that tells everyone about something
refugee	a homeless person
sponsor	to support someone, often for charity
Suffragette Movement	a group, mainly women, who wanted votes for women
tomboy	a girl who prefers to play boy's games and sports
try/tried	to find out if someone is guilty of a crime
United Nations	an international group working for peace in the world
university	a place where people study after leaving school
vote	to choose someone
wage (war)	to fight a war
war correspondent	a newspaper reporter who writes about wars and battles

Index

Notes for parents and teachers

It is a sad fact that the work of The Save the Children Fund, or Save the Children as it is known today, is never out of the news. There is hardly a news bulletin on the television that does not mention some disaster or war somewhere in the world where the work of Save the Children is needed or is already being carried out.

Consequently, most children today grow up with an awareness of the world's problems that was probably lacking in the general outlook of their parents and grandparents and, surely, this is no bad thing. All the more reason, therefore, that the dedication of people such as Eglantyne Jebb should be remembered.

Further information about Eglantyne Jebb's life, the history of Save the Children, and the work the organisation carries out today can be found on the Save the Children website at www.savethechildren.org.uk or www.savethechildren.net.